The Life and Death of
ELVIS PRESLEY

THE KING'S EARLY YEARS
TEENAGE YEARS
THE BEGINNING
THE BIG MOVIES
IN THE ARMY
HIS MOTHER'S DEATH
HIS LOVES
HIS CO-STARS
"ELVIS THE PELVIS"
THE BIG SUCCESS
THE HIT RECORDS
THE IMITATORS
HIS LATER YEARS
ELVIS: BIG BUSINESS
THE KING IS DEAD
THE FINAL GOODBYE
HOW HIS MUSICAL PEERS SAW HIM

HARRISON HOUSE

Copyright© 1977 by Manor Books, Inc.   Printed in U.S.A.
Published under arrangement with Ottenheimer Publishers, Inc.

THE KING'S EARLY YEARS

On August 18, 1977, every last flag in Memphis, Tennessee was flying at half mast. The town of Memphis, as well as the rest of the world, was in mourning for Elvis Presley, the undisputed king of rock music, who died on Tuesday, August sixteenth, at the age of 42, but not before he left behind a virtual legacy of records, films and just about anything else.

If the passing of "Elvis the Pelvis" makes us all feel a little older, it's only because we are. Old institutions like Elvis Presley however, are not supposed to die.

From his first big hit, *Heartbreak Hotel*, right up to *Moody Blue*, his last, Elvis never once faded from public view. His fans, most of whom grew up on Elvis, remain undyingly loyal to this very day, and always will. Aside from being one of the most successful, influential and controversial entertainers the history of show business, he was also one of the best. Even in his later years, when his weight started to balloon, the mobs turned out to see and hear him and blissfully ignored it when his tight satin pants would split down the seam due to his excessive weight.

It was a less than spectacular start for the young Presley. It was almost as if the odds were against him from the start. His beginnings, as might have been expected, were a little less than modest. His parents, Vernon and Gladys, were simple folk from Mississippi and made no qualms about it. Home for them was a two room shack in a tiny hamlet called Tupelo, some two hundred miles from anywhere. Vernon was a factory worker in those days.

Best Wishes
Elvis Presley

On January 8, 1935, Gladys Presley, formerly Smith, gave birth to twins, Elvis Aron came first, followed by Jesse. Jesse, unfortunately died a few hours later,

The weak infant that eventually would go on to become one of the biggest show business personalities of all time lay sick and feeble for some seven days before the warning signals were finally shut off.

Elvis' mother, Gladys, was convinced of her son's musical talent long before he cut his first disk. "When Elvis was just a little

Top: Gladys Presley seems less than thrilled at Elvis's army stint.

Middle: One last kiss before leaving.

Bottom: Vernon Presley is no more thrilled than his wife.

fellow," she once said, "not more than two years old, he would slide off my lap (in church) run down the aisle and scramble up to the platform. He would stand looking at the choir and trying to sing with them. He was too little to know the words, but even then he could carry a tune." His voice, even then, declare those who remember him, had that certain hint of rhythm, timing and tune. Shocked by young Elvis' behavior however, Gladys scuttled after him, retrieved him and scolded him for committing the deadly sin of disrupting a good service in

the First Assembly Church of God.

It wasn't until he was twelve however, that his talent showed true signs. His father bought him a guitar, Elvis' first, for the sum of $12.95, paltry today but in 1947 a sizable amount for a factory worker. "He liked the guitar the best of all his things," Gladys once remarked. "He'd sit in front of the radio, picking out melodies, or sometimes he'd play the phonograph trying to learn the songs he heard."

What neither the young Elvis or his parents knew was that

and teachers alike as friendly and easygoing. There seemed to be little really outstanding in Elvis, except maybe a better-than-average interest in music. Whatever he had, though, went unnoticed for some time to come.

1954 brought graduation from L.C. Hume High School. Shortly afterwards, curiosity seemed to get the better of Elvis. He journeyed to a small recording studio, where for four dollars he got to make two numbers. The songs, *My Happiness* and *That's When Your Heartaches Begin*, were intended as a present to his

unusual. He also promised to call Elvis sometime. Delighted, Elvis rushed home and promptly forgot all about it.

A few months later, Elvis started working as a truck driver at $35 a week. It was a step up from usher at a movie theater, for which he earned about half the amount. Sam Phillips, along about the same time, kept to his word and called Elvis, inviting him to Sun Label to cut a record.

The names of Bill Monroe and Arthur "Big Boy" Crudup mean nothing to most people, but they were quite important in influenc-

Left and right: Vernon Presley and his only son mourn the death of their wife and mother.

there was gold in them hills. Elvis, at the time, had no true ambitions to become a star but rather his main goal, according to an interviewer some ten years ago, was "to be somebody and to feel like somebody."

This did not include being a superstar though. Elvis was totally unaware of what he could really achieve, and ultimately did.

It was off to Memphis, lock, stock and barrel in 1948, when Elvis was thirteen. He attended L.C. Hume High School, where he was remembered by students

mother.

"Sounds like somebody beatin' on a trash lid," Elvis late said of the crude recordings. The engineer at the studio however, thought more of Elvis potential than he obviously did. The engineer happened to be Sam Phillips, who was then starting his own recording company called Sun, which launched the careers of Johnny Cash, Jerry Lee Lewis, but most importantly, Elvis Presley. Though his company was still in its infancy stages, Phillips liked what he heard. He complimented Elvis, claiming that his voice was

ing young Elvis, whose singles for Phillips were written and recorded by the aforementioned singers. *Blue Moon of Kentucky* was a bluegrass ballad written by Bill Monroe and eventually ended up being recorded by Elvis on one side of the disk he made for Phillips. On the other side was *That's All Right, Mama*, a blues standard written by Big Boy' Crudup and was the biggest influence on Elvis at the time, helping him mold his style.

It was a mixture of white country music and blues that made Elvis stand out, as his form of

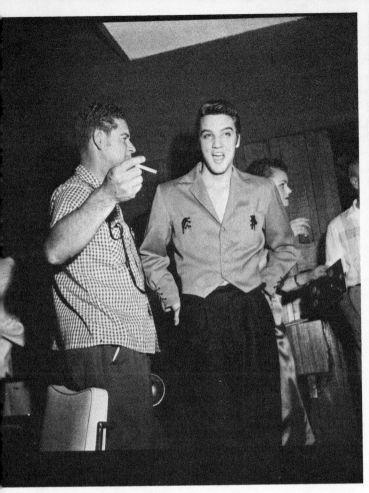

Top left and right: The King enjoys a
night on the town.

music had never really been
heard before. His first disk for
Phillips was quite a hit—so much
so that Phillips had to scramble to
catch up with a back order for
some six thousand records of Elvis' crooning, no less than one
week after the record was released.

"When I found Elvis, he had
nothing but a million dollars
worth of talent," says Colonel
Tom Parker. Parker, a one time
carnival barker, was one of the
first to sit up and take notice at
Presley's record. It was Parker
that saw something marketable
in Presley and started him on the
road to success, true success. The
rest, as anyone knows, is history.

Bottom right: When Elvis hit it big,
getting women was no problem.

TEENAGE YEARS

While a sex symbol at twenty-two, the years preceeding it were less than easy for Elvis, who found high school in particular one long obstacle course. Presley's longtime bodyguard and friend, Red West, who was one year behind Elvis in high school, remembers, "It seems that the way I remembered him, someone was always picking on him. He was easy going enough, quiet, well mannered, was always respectful to his elders and he never wised off to anyone. In a lot of ways, he was a lot nicer than some of the others around."

It wasn't Elvis' mouth that was arrogant, but rather, but his ap-

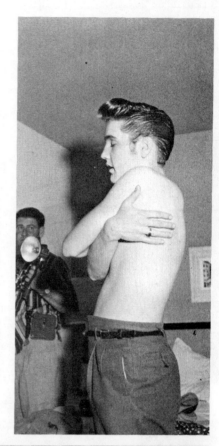

pearance. Friends remember him spending hours in the bathroom at school combing his ducktail to perfection. He was usually clad in a leather jacket and jeans, but when he wasn't, it was even worse, usually a colored pair of pegged pants. In the deep south, where ninety-nine percent of the students at H.L. Hume High School were little less than albino, Elvis stood out the way Sammy Davis Jr. would stand out at a Ku Klux Klan cookout.

"It was the hair," says Red West. "It always got him into all kinds of trouble. Had he had a regular haircut like the rest of us, he probably wouldn't have been

Right and below: Pres changes into his party duds.

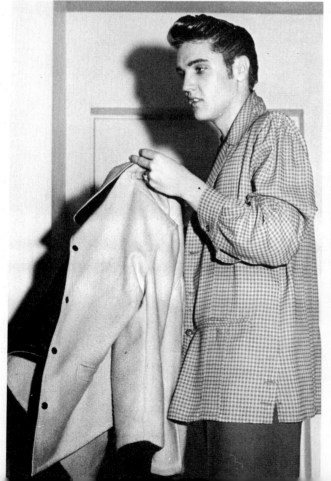

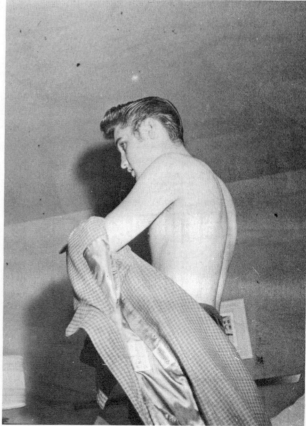

Above: Elvis the Pelvis turns on the juice.

bothered. I guess the older kids thought he was trying to show off or something. The hair, though, has always been his crown of glory. I have never known any other human to take more time over his hair. He would spend hours on it, smoothing, mussing it up and combing it—and combing it again!"

Perhaps in an attempt to become accepted by his peers, Elvis tried out for the high school football team, but with little less than dismal results. Had he a bit more weight, not to mention confidence, the results might have been different. "Elvis lasted on the squad about three weeks," said Red West. "The coach couldn't stand him and his long hair. He was always on Elvis about cutting his hair and shamed him so much that he finally left the squad altogether!"

Every year at Hume High, a variety show would be held to raise money for those students that needed it, for books, football gear or whatever. Determined, yet still shy, Elvis showed up, the battered guitar strapped over his shoulder. From the first note he played, Elvis was the winner, as girls and women teachers alike swooned at his throaty renditions. From then on, during the last half of his senior year, Elvis was now "in." He found himself accepted, finally, by his classmates and also by those who had at one time scorned him for his slightly unusual appearance. He went to all the parties though, and usually had to be induced to sing a song or two.

Graduating from H.C. Hume seemed to be the end of his singing career, at least for the time being. Elvis was just as content to work full time, driving a truck. He landed a job with the Crown Electrical Company, driving a truck for $1.25 an hour. Elvis was happy as a truck driver; indeed, coming from near poverty as he had, a steady income and a little security went a long way. Singing however, was never that far from his mind.

THE BEGINNINGS

While driving for the Crown Electrical Company, Elvis would, in his daily travels, pass by the Sun Recording Company, operated by a man named Sam Phillips. The Sun Recording Company was new in those days, but Phillips had big aspirations, which did blossom.

There was a gimmick Phillips used in his business to bring in a little extra revenue. For four dollars, anyone could make their own recording, be it a birthday greeting or whatever. The concept itself is far from new; similar recording booths were to be found all over the country. For a quarter, one could make a record, say or do anything for three minutes.

Elvis made a mental note about the offer, and one Saturday afternoon he wandered in to make a recording for his mother's birthday. It was quite fortunate that Marion Keisker was working that day, for had she not, Elvis might have remained a truck driver. Miss Keisker was always on the lookout for new, fresh talent and was more than willing to give it a helping hand. Many credit Sam Phillips with discovering Elvis, but he himself knew the real truth: it was Marion Keisker. Being Phillip's office manager, she knew better than anyone what Phillips was looking for—mainly, a black voice in a white body.

When Elvis paid the four dollars to make the recording for his mother, little did he know that fame and fortune were waiting for him just around the corner. Marion liked what she heard after Elvis made the recording, so much so that she recorded from his recording so that her boss,

Above: Mobbed by adoring fans as usual.

Phillips could hear Elvis sing.

Phillips listened to the recordings with mild interest. Presley, he said, was sort of what he was looking for but not quite. Still, Phillips was more congenial than most and gave Elvis a boost most young performers never got. He teamed him with two somewhat accomplished musicians named Scotty Moore, who played the piano and guitar, and Bill Black, who was a bass player. Together, with Phillips, they formed a group called the Starlight Wranglers. Neither Moore nor Black was heavily impressed with Elvis, who was not singing the way he wanted to, but rather,

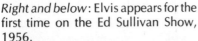

Right and below: Elvis appears for the first time on the Ed Sullivan Show, 1956.

singing the way he thought the others wanted him to.

One afternoon, Elvis, along with Moore and Black, were sitting around and shooting the breeze. Suddenly, as if a gust of wind had propelled him, Elvis picked up his guitar and started banging out a rendition of Arthur Crudup's *That's Alright, Mama*. Crudup was a black blues singer who Elvis later credited for influencing him.

Though Elvis claimed that his rendition of *That's Alright, Mama* sounded like someone beating the lid of a garbage can, Phillips liked what he heard and had the trio make a recording of the song. Less than a week later, Phillips, in the true tradition of the song plugger, sold it around town to disk jockeys and the like. The year 1954, however, was not a banner year for black-white relations, and Elvis's voice sounded heavily black, which provided Phillips with his first obstacle. Despite that, however, the record sold some seven thousand copies, a nice figure in those days. But it wouldn't have sold as well had it not been for Dewey Phillips (no relation to Sam), a local DJ in Memphis then. Phillips urged Dewey to play the song on his program, and despite Dewey's reservations, he played the record nonetheless. It brought Elvis minor stardom.

By the end of 1954, however, Elvis was more or less where he'd been all his life—down. He was still working for the Crown Electrical Company and still giving most of his earnings to his mother. Nothing much seemed to happen, except maybe for a local gig here and there.

Bob Neal, like Dewey Phillips, was a local disk jockey who took an immediate liking to Elvis Presley and took over the position as his manager. Neal was in big demand at high school dances and the like, and his local contacts proved worthwhile.

During all of this, though, was about the time Elvis started to develop his style of singing a song—swaying hips and all. Elvis, according to Red Smith, got more pleasure out of singing gospel songs than anything else, and it was during these occasional lapses of singing them that his gyrations began to take form, naturally.

Elvis got less than unanimous applause when, toward the end of 1954, he was playing small clubs and restaurants. He was received politely, with light but unspectacular applause. Also around this time, Elvis teamed with Red West, his high school chum. West wasn't a musician or anything but rather a friend, one of Elvis' few. He invited Red to join him in late 1954 or early 1955 on the road, as driver, companion, and, as it turned out, bodyguard. Elvis was still having problems with his appearance, and while Memphis may have accepted him, outlying areas had yet to learn the Presley mysticism.

Elvis, along with Scotty Moore and Bill Black, not to mention Bob Neal's help, formed another trio called The Blue Moon Boys. Neal's early morning radio show had a radius of two hundred miles, a considerable distance in those days. Through the show, the Blue Moon Boys were hired for local as well as out of town gigs. Anything and anywhere was fair game, from Church auditoriums to high school auditoriums to gyms and schoolhouses. Through Neal and *Billboard*, which was then and still is the Bible of the recording industry, The Blue Moon Boys were soon on their way. Their appeal was growing, and not just in Tennessee. Louisiana, Florida, Alabama and Mississippi were also states they played in. Elvis was making up to two hundred dollars a week at this time, most of which he sent home to his folks, for whom he had an un-dying loyalty, and always did, until his last days.

Elvis was slowly becoming an idol in the deep south, although

Above: Rehearsing for an upcoming stint on the Sullivan Show.

in New York and Los Angeles, the big recording studios and agents had still to take notice. Through Bob Neal's careful, as well as honest, managing, Elvis and the Blue Moon Boys were rapidly achieving status. Elvis was without a doubt the true star of the group, and even then had girls swooning when he opened his mouth.

Neal thought it important to impress it upon the New York and Los Angeles boys that Elvis wasn't just another "hillbilly singer." Neal stressed the importance of a national appearance. Presley, he claimed, not only had good looks, but an impressive singing voice and professional backup.

Through hook and crook, Neal arranged an appearance for Elvis,

rather an audition for an appearance, on *The Arthur Godfrey Show*. Elvis and The Blue Moon Boys were certain that the big time awaited them and the huge cash offers would start rolling in, no longer would they have to drive two or three hundred miles for a one night stand.

They were wrong. Elvis and The Blue Moon Boys went through their entire repetoire, only to be beaten down by those "dam Yankees." As everyone knows, the casting department made a serious mistake turning down Elvis and the Blue Moon Boys.

They flew home, dejected, but not discouraged. Fame still awaited Elvis, but not yet. Not before Colonel Tom Parker entered the scene.

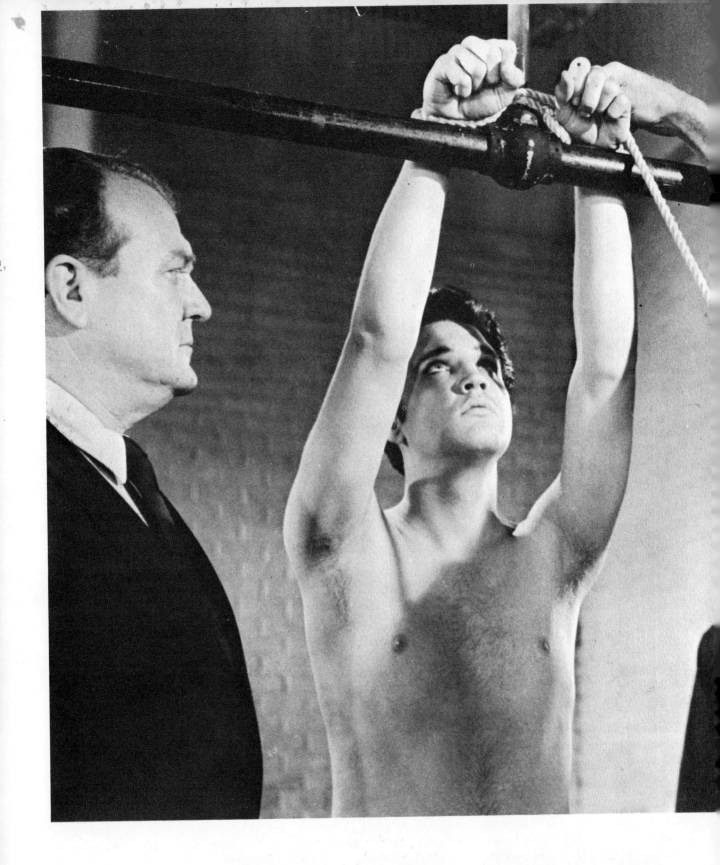

THE BIG

Jailhouse Rock

Love Me Tender

Charro

MOVIES

Love Me Tender

1957 could be viewed as a turning point in Elvis' career, not to mention his life.

While Elvis was touring the country that year, Colonel Tom Parker was working elsewhere, in Tinseltown, Hollywood, U.S.A., negotiating a picture deal for his red-hot property.

Hal Wallis, who today is well into his seventies and still going strong, was serving as producer for Paramount Pictures. Wallis was one of the shrewder men in the business, and not unlike Colonel Tom Parker, knew an asset when he saw one. Wallis, it might be added, also saw the boxoffice earning potential in a comedy team called Martin and Lewis, around 1948. They are, of course, Dean Martin and Jerry Lewis, and while Wallis didn't exactly discover them, he did have the foresight to bring them back to Hollywood, where from 1949 up until their splitup in 1956, they helped keep Paramount in the black.

Paramount too was, in 1956, undergoing the strains all movie studios faced with the advent of the idiot box, as television was called. More than ever before the studios were looking for a hot property.

Elvis was, according to friends, ecstatic about making his first movie, a minor yarn entitled *Love Me Tender*. The story wasn't much, but then, until he made his last film in 1969, the plots of Elvis Presley movies never did have much going for them. Wallis wisely knew that Elvis's movies would have to be tailored especially for him, to suit his image. Also, to view his earlier films today, one imagines if maybe the screenwriters left blank pages in their scripts to accommodate the many songs that dotted Elvis's movies.

Upon the release of *Love Me Tender*, both Presley and Colonel Parker truly struck it rich. RCA, with Paramount, originated what was called "the package deal." Basically, the concept worked

Jailhouse Rock

like this: release the songs from the movie on an album and clean up. Simple enough, to be sure, but the deal always made millions for everyone involved.

Presley's leading lady in *Love Me Tender* was Debra Paget, who also starred in *The Ten Commandments*, Cecille B. DeMille's Biblical extravaganza the year before. It was during the filming of *Love Me Tender*, according to Red West, that Elvis developed a huge crush on his pretty co-star.

Loving You

Miss Paget however, did not obviously feel the same way toward the movie newcomer that Elvis felt about her. She regarded him as "a nice kid" and that was about it. Then again, in all fairness, Miss Paget was dating someone with a bit more influence in those days—Howard Hughes.

1957 offered Elvis in *Jailhouse Rock*, a simple tale of a simple man in the slammer. The film, which co-starred Mickey Shaughnessey, had Elvis as Vince, a young man who goes to jail after accidentally killing another man in a barroom brawl. It is in prison that he meets Hank Houghton, himself a onetime western singer. During a jailhouse concert Hunk is convinced of his cellmate's talent. Hunk, no dummy, signs Vince to a longterm contract. Both parties naturally forget about it until the day they meet as free men. Vince however, has made it big by this time, although his head has swelled considerably by this time.

Honoring the contract though, Vince takes Hunk on as a go-fer. Only then, with the help of Peggy Van Alden, a song plugger, does Vince see the error of his ways and become nice again.

Jailhouse Rock, like Elvis' previous two films, were box office smashes, a trend that was to continue well into the sixties. In fact, as far as moneymaking films go, Elvis is the champ. Not one of his films lost money, a claim that most movie stars, from Brando to Laurence Olivier, can't make.

Despite this, Elvis was still unhappy about his films in later life. He would grow disgusted at what he would see on the late show sometimes. He once confessed: "Who is that fast-talking hillbilly that nobody can understand? One day he is singing to a dog, then to a car, then to a cow. They are all the same damned movies with that Southerner just singing to something different."

1958 was not the greatest year of Presley's life, as things turned out.

Elvis with the ever-present sneer that
ultimately becomes a trademark.

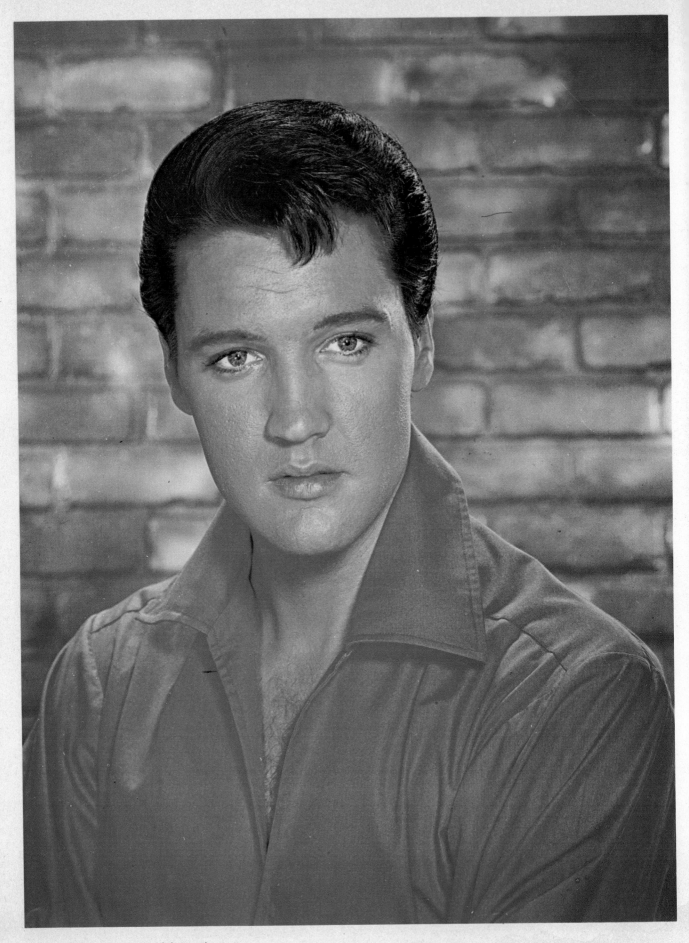

A Presley Portrait of the early sixties, right before his film career got started.

He was one of the first to use an electric guitar.

Elvis and the "Vitalis" look.

Elvis and Nancy Sinatra in *Speedway*.

G.I. Blues

Kid Galahad
Speedway

Kissin' Cousins
Stay Away, Joe

Spinout

Viva Las Vegas

Girl Happy

Harum Scarum

Easy Come, Easy Go

Change of Habit

Tickle Me

It All Happened At the World's Fair

Double Trouble

IN THE ARMY

1958 brought Elvis his biggest money deal to date: for starring in *King Creole* for Paramouth, Elvis would get some five hundred thousand dollars, and fifty percent of the profits. Quite tidy, by today's standards, much less 1958 standards.

The film was based loosely on a Harold Robbin's book, *A Stone for Danny*.

Filming *King Creole* was not the highlight of 1958, however. That year, Elvis signed on with yet another employer, namely, the U.S. Army. When word of Elvis' draft got around, the U.S. Army had second thoughts about Mr. Presley. Induction centers and recruiting depots were picketed by thousands of protesting women, who were totally convinced that the Army was putting The King's life in grave danger. Letters poured in from all over the country, trying to block the army career of Elvis Presley. Politicians from all over the country began to comment on the situation, eager to get newspaper coverage.

Despite some hostility, the entire affair was light and somewhat good natured. Elvis himself was the first to calm the masses by saying, "All I want is to be treated as a regular G.I. I want to do my duty and I'm mighty proud to be given the opportunity to serve my country."

But there was another fly in the ointment. For one thing, some three hundred thousand dollars had already been spent toward the filming of *King Creole*. Should Presley, according to Hal Wallis, report to the induction center when he was supposed to, the film would have to be scrapped altogether.

Elvis put in for a deferment. Deferments were quite regular in those days, as most young men were in college or finishing school. With Elvis however, the situation was a little different, so much so tha State Representative Nick Johnson, from Harlan County, Kentucky, resigned from the draft board with the claim "I cannot conscienciously ask any mountain boy to serve the country unless afforded the same treatment as Mr. Presley."

Despite this, Elvis' deferment was granted and the film was finally completed. Oddly, the film ranks as one of Elvis' best acting efforts, a cut above the rest of his films.

On March 24, 1958, Elvis reported to the Memphis draft board, accompanied by his mother Gladys and his father, Vernon.

Newspaper reporters from all over the world, from Canada to Australia, were on hand to witness Presley's induction. They bombarded him with questions, such as "would you wear combat boots?", "would you sing while marching to boost morale?", "Would you ask fans to send you fried chicken?" Through it all, though, Elvis was polite and well mannered, as he usually was.

During all of this, Colonel Parker was not far from the proceedings. In fact, he was busy handing out photos, eight by ten glossies of The King. Parker, said Red West, never missed a beat.

Presley soon became Private Presley, U.S. 53310761. He was

Top, middle, bottom and upper right:
Elvis "The King" Presley was just as
popular among the youths of Germany as he was in the United States.

sent to Fort Chaffee in Arkansas. As the camp barber shaved off Elvis' locks that fateful day, Colonel Parker commented, "I know a lot of people that would pay a lot of money for that hair."

Elvis may have disliked army life, but no one could have ever accused him of cursing the darkness and not lighting a candle. To make sure he had all the comforts of home, Elvis rented a four room house in the town of Kileen, near Fort Hood, where he was later stationed. In it, he put his mother, father, grandmother and assorted friends, who would drop by at any time during the day or night.

Elvis was due to leave for Germany after basic training. He was also planning to take his entourage with him, that was until the day came that was to change his life forever, and haunt him for the remaining years of his life.

Above: Elvis and some of his older but still adoring fans.

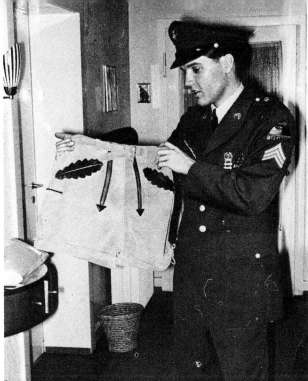

Above: Elvis during his Army stint in Germany.

Left: Pres packs his trunk before shipping out.
Above: To this day, Elvis still has many loyal fans in Germany.

Left: Elvis signs an autograph for a grateful fan.

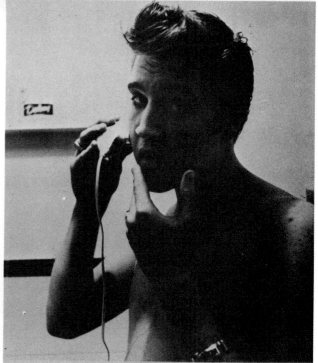

Above: Though a superstar at twenty-two, Elvis shaved only every *other* day.

HIS MOTHER'S DEATH

Gladys Presley was a sensitive, caring mother to her only child, Elvis. Few people know that Elvis' twin brother Jesse died stillborn; taking into account that Gladys almost died giving birth to Elvis at the same time, it's no wonder why he was so dedicated to his mother, and she loved him so much in return.

Gladys Presley married young, at nineteen, as was the tradition in the deep South in the year 1934. The following year, she gave birth to Elvis.

Elvis once said that his mother had the strength of a salmon fighting its way upstream, the soft looks of a doe and was a loving mother. Elvis's friends remember that she was a bit overprotective, but Gladys saw it differently. Elvis had been spared, whereas Jesse had not. Gladys dedicated her life to Elvis' well being.

Oddly enough, both Gladys and Elvis were the same age when they met their deaths; forty-two.

In July of 1958, the family noticed a change in Gladys. Whereas she was usually energetic, she had seemed to have lost her spark, her charge.

It was decided that she and Vernon return to Memphis so that Gladys could see a doctor. No one seemed overly concerned; Gladys was strong, only forty-two, and had years to go. Or so they thought.

It was diagnosed as hepatitis. Elvis got emergency leave and flew (despite his terror of flying) back to Memphis to be at his mother's bedside.

He remained there for some thirty-six hours, not sleeping. At midnight, and at Vernon's request, Elvis went home to get some rest. Three hours later, his father called with the news: his mother had died of a heart attack.

Elvis arrived, barely, at the hospital in a state of heavy shock. He threw himself across his mother's bed and sobbed uncontrollably.

He could barely talk to news-

men that were at the scene. At her funeral, Vernon had had a famous gospel group called The Blackwood Brothers to sing. Elvis was still in shock.

He erected a huge monument at the Memphis cemetery at Forest Lawn. Whenever Elvis was in Memphis, he would go to the cemetery to pay his respects.

One of his friends during his army days was Nick Adams, quite an accomplished actor but never truly appreciated by Hollywood. Adams, who later committed suicide, was a close friend of Presley's at one time and would often hang around Elvis' rented home while he was stationed at Ford Hood.

Elvis had been in the Second Armored Division, but pretty soon his unit was to make up a replacement in Germany of the Third Armored Division which was General Patton's old outfit. Before long, Elvis was on his way to Germany.

HIS LOVES

Presley always kept Priscilla on a pedestal. It was as if he got what he wanted and put it away in storage, and went on to something else. Priscilla could have anything she wanted, but the thing she wanted most was Elvis. In the last couple of years she was with him, he was away from her eighty-five percent of the time. They would spend the weekend together and then he was off again. She could buy all the clothes and jewels she wanted and Elvis would not have said a word, but she didn't want that. She was not a heavy spender when you think of other girls who have been around him. She just wanted a normal life. But toward the end, Elvis' life consisted of staying in bed all day. There were times when she couldn't see him for a week. He would just stay up in his room taking downers, watching television, and watching the closed circuit television which covered the entire house. She didn't want that kind of life. Toward the end she wanted to do something with her days, get out and enjoy life. She didn't want to stay in a hotel room all day or the bedroom of Graceland all day, asleep.

He tried to keep his affairs from Priscilla, fiercely denying any gossip. Even though it was true, he didn't want to hurt Priscilla. He was very convincing, because by the time the columnists got onto a story about a girl he was seeing, he would be back in Memphis, and he would turn it around that these columnists had him out with a girl while he was at Priscilla's side. When she was younger, she swallowed it, not so much later on.

Above: Priscilla Ann Beaulieu at twenty-two, right before she changed her last name to Presley by marrying Elvis.

Then, one day, she finally tired of the whole thing. If Mr. and Mrs. Elvis Presley had been the subjects of countless fan magazines, it was just the beginning. Priscilla ran off with karate teacher Mike Stone. Elvis swore revenge and even dispatched his bodyguards to eliminate Stone.

They didn't, of course.

Priscilla was no longer a little girl, no longer naive as she had once been. She knew what she wanted, whether Elvis liked it or not.

No matter how many women Elvis had in his past, there was only one woman he really ever loved. Priscilla Beaulieu Presley. They both had a genuine love for each other, and even though she left Presley for another man, no other man had as lasting an influence in her growth as Elvis Presley. After all the glossy fan magazine pictures and stories are digested it must be remembered

Above: Mr. and Mrs. Presley right after they tied the knot.

Left: Many claim Elvis married Priscilla because she reminded him of his late mother.

Above: Elvis and Priscilla shortly after their honeymoon.

Below: Priscilla smiles despite rumors of marital strife.

that Presley virtually raised Priscilla from the time she was a fifteen-year-old schoolgirl until they finally split in an explosion of anger, selfishness and misunderstanding.

Presley met Priscilla in Germany, in the closing months of his army service. He talked about her, which was something unheard of according to Presley's friends.

No matter how many girls Elvis was seeing he always talked about his little girl in Germany. He made several long distance phone calls to her, and to the close friends around Presley it was obvious he was finally in love.

Elvis arranged for Priscilla, daughter of an Air Force captain who was later to become a colonel, to visit him over Christmas, 1960. He wanted to see just

whether he was indeed in love, or whether he was just infatuated by a fresh and beautiful schoolgirl.

After his return to Germany, Elvis knew he couldn't go on living in the states without her. He started to make arrangements to have her come back. He spent a lot of time talking to her father on the telephone, telling him that he needed her, loved her and would respect her in every way that her father wanted her respected. He told him that he would marry her one day, and he undertook to put her through school.

He was sure Priscilla was the one he wanted because she was better than any of the girls he was running around with in Hollywood.

Priscilla lived with Presley's parents, and since she was Catholic was enrolled at the school of the Immaculate Con-

Above: Vernon Presley seems to enjoy his son's success.

Right: Priscilla's younger brother, Tommy Beaulieu.

ception, which the boys used to call "Virginity Row."

As soon as Priscilla was old enough to drive, Presley bought her a Corvair and then a lavender Chevy sports coupe. She lived in a mansion, she had the best schooling, everything money could buy, and the sex symbol of all sex symbols as her romancer. What more could she want? As the years went on and Priscilla's personality developed, she found there was much more in life than just riches. She was, she realized, right up until 1972 a virtual prisoner in a gilded cage.

HIS CO-STARS

When an individual plunked down a dollar or two for an Elvis Presley movie, he usually didn't expect more than a simple story, some light comedy, and last, but not least, a bevy of pretty girls. He was rarely disappointed, as there was always a well stocked commodity of curvaceous blondes and brunettes in his films. After all, there had to be something for the men in the audience as well.

Love Me Tender co-starred a great beauty of the fifties, Debra Paget. Elvis reportedly developed a crush on Miss Paget during the filming. His affection, however, was not returned by her.

Where Miss Paget is these days is anyone's guess. Most of the women who appeared with Elvis were subject to immediate stardom, but for the most part, it was fleeting.

True, some of Elvis' female co-stars went on to bigger and better things. For instance, Ann-Margaret appeared with him in *Viva Las Vegas*, which was a big hit. But she had more to offer except just another pretty face.

Donna Douglas was the love interest in *Frankie and Johnny*. Before vanishing into the woodwork as well, Miss Douglas went on to co-star, along with Buddy Ebsen, Irene Ryan and Max Baer

Above: Elvis chats with Shirley Mac-Laine on the Paramount lot, 1960.

Above: Presley and Priscilla Taurog, daughter of director Norman Taurog, who directed six of Elvis's films.

Below: Elvis is given a screaming sendoff as he leaves for Hawaii.

Below: The King gets a lift with Barbara Stanwyck during the filming of *Roustabout*.

Right: The famous sneer, Natalie Wood seems dazed.

Jr. in *The Beverly Hillbillies*, which could be classified as bigger, although not necessarily better.

Shelley Fabares appeared in *Speedway* with Elvis, and certainly held her head above water, with a string of television series that lasted well into the Seventies. Miss Fabares, however, is known mainly for her work on *The Donna Reed Show*, in which she played the eldest daughter to Donna Reed and television hubby Carl Betz. Betz and Miss Fabares also appeared in *Speedway* together.

Speedway, made in 1965, also marked the last film for veteran comedienne Una Merkel, whose early films include *The Bank Dick*, where she played opposite W.C. Fields. Miss Merkel also starred in *Destry Rides Again*, with Marlene Deitrich and James Stewart.

Mary Tyler Moore also managed to serve time in a Presley film entitled *Change of Habit*. Mary Tyler Moore, as most people know, went on to score, first opposite Dick Van Dyke in *The Dick Van Dyke Show*, and later her own series, *The Mary Tyler Moore Show*. Aside from having her own television production agency, it can be assumed that Miss Moore did somewhat better than most of the women Presley co-starred with.

Whatever the outcome, Presley films were rarely ever boring.

The Pelvis goes straight—with a pinstripe suit.

In the sixties, Elvis' film image changed with the times.

A super-slick Elvis starred
in *Speedway*, 1965.

He always hated it when his hair
got messed-up.

The Prez in 1966—still going strong and showing no signs of slowing down.

Elvis and co-star Nancy Sinatra in the climax of *Speedway*.

As Elvis and Nancy demonstrate, styles *have* changed a lot.

Presley with electric guitar and Nancy Sinatra—her boots were made for walking.

In their only movie together, Nancy Sinatra looks star-struck.

Elvis, in his past *Jailhouse Rock* days.

An older, more distinguished looking Presley in 1968.

Elvis and Ann-Margret rehearsing.

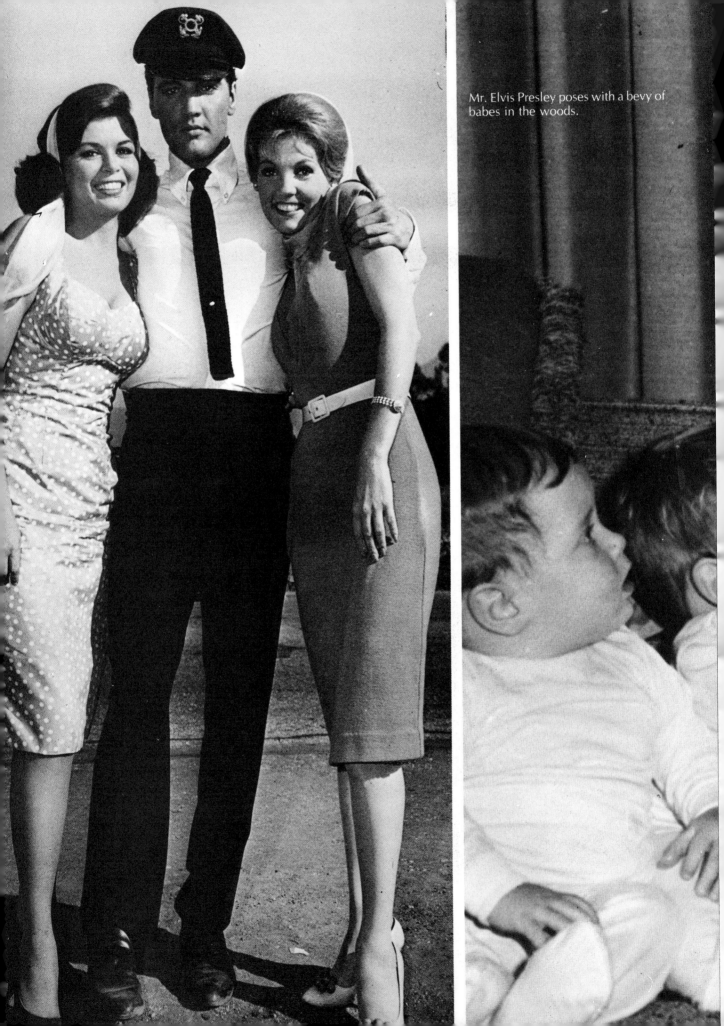

Mr. Elvis Presley poses with a bevy of babes in the woods.

"ELVIS THE PELVIS"

Above and left: Presley right before his world tour in 1972.

Colonel Tom Parker was perhaps the biggest element in Elvis' success. A grizzled, no-nonsense veteran of show business, Parker started out by working for his uncle, along about 1927 or 1928, as a barker at a carnival. Parker came up the ranks the hard way, but not before he learned what made a fast buck.

In 1934, Parker quit his uncle's circus for bigger and better things. He struck out on his own as a press agent and publicity man when he discovered that there were fortunes to be reaped. In his later years, Parker's motto was, "never mind what they say about you, as long as they spell the name right."

A young Eddy Arnold, who later went on to become one of the biggest names in Country & Western music, hired Parker as his press agent early in both their respective careers. Arnold heard through friends that Parker was a driven man who always got the desired results.

Arnold and Parker split in 1951 or thereabouts, and it wasn't until 1954 that he managed to latch on to another up-and-coming talent, Hank Snow, also a big name in the C&W world.

Along about the same time, Elvis was still under contract to

Sam Phillips. Phillips was a shrewd businessman. With a handful of hot disks behind Elvis, Phillip's felt certain that "the kid" was ready for the big time. He went to Randy Wood, head of Dot Records, one of the bigger record companies of the time. Wood liked Elvis but was convinced that he was nothing more than "a flash in the pan." What's more, Wood already had a hot prospect that year—named Pat Boone!

Oscar Davis, at the same time, was praising Elvis highly, convinced that he was a hot property. Davis also worked closely with Colonel Parker, and although Parker trusted Davis's judgement, he still was skeptical.

Elvis, at the time, was appearing at the Louisiana Hayride, a concert hall in the tradition of the Grand Ole Opry. He was a sensation there, and it wasn't until Parker caught Elvis there that he was convinced of Davis' sincerity.

Parker, forever the shrewd businessman, knew he had something hot and marketable in Elvis. As he later explained it, Elvis was the first male singer to use sex as a part of his style. Up until then, claimed Parker, women singers were sexy, but never males. They were a lot of things: romantic, heroic, sad or inspiring, but never sexy.

Parker liked what he saw—Elvis seemed to be a young woman's dream-kind of rebel when he appeared onstage. But offstage, he was polite and easygoing, a truly rare commodity.

Elvis, at this time, was still under contract to Bob Neal, but not for long. Neal was well aware that Elvis was growing in stature

as a performer, and there was little reason to stick it out in Memphis any longer. He allowed Parker to take over and manage Elvis' career solely, which Parker did, to the hilt.

Randy Wood of Dot Record, who refused to buy Elvis' contract, must have been tearing his hair out for the blunder he made. Parker promptly sold Elvis' contract to RCA Records, and in less than three months he cut his first disk for them, a little ditty called *Heartbreak Hotel*. Though it sounded like it had been recorded in an echo chamber, the recording sold more than a million copies, a phenomenal amount in those days. Either way, Elvis was on his way.

After releasing four of Elvis' past hits, RCA had Elvis record *I Want You, I Need You, I Love You*, which also proved to be a million record seller.

In 1956, through Parker's ingenuity, Elvis was The King. At this time, RCA handed him a five thousand dollar bonus, which he used to buy a Cadillac for his mother.

Above: Pres at thirty-four and still going strong.

THE BIG SUCCESS

According to Red West, 1956 was the year everything took off, and "everything Elvis touched turned to gold."

Through Parker's shrewd judgement and know-how, Elvis was launched. In New York City however, the reaction was quite different. Ed Sullivan, who had his hour-long variety show at the time, proclaimed that he would rather run a sixty minute test pattern than feature Elvis Presley on his show.

Parker was determined to make New York eat their words.

Many people today believe that it was Ed Sullivan who gave Presley his first shot at national TV, but this is not exactly so. In 1956, Jackie Gleason of *The Honeymooners* fame, was producing a summer replacement show that featured Tommy and Jimmy Dorsey, broadcast from the CBS theatre in midtown Manhattan. Through Parker's pushing and urging, Gleason finally consented to feature Elvis on his Dorsey Brothers show, which, at the time, was floundering badly in the ratings, being up against a heavy contender at the time, *The Perry Como Show*.

On a snowy Saturday evening in January, 1956, Elvis, along with Scotty Moore and Bill Black, ventured into the studio at CBS. All were well aware that it was a do-or-die effort, that if they didn't impress the CBS brass, it was back to Memphis and The Blue Mountain Boys. Also, Colonel Parker had arranged for Elvis to get an unheard of twelve

Elvis and pretty fan at Las Vegas.

hundred dollars apiece for six appearances, a huge amount for a guest shot in the earlier days of television. The studio audience, it might be pointed out, was of little value, as the studio was but half filled.

When the time came, Elvis slipped into a heartfelt rendition of *Heartbreak Hotel*, complete with swinging hips, sneer and gyrations. Then, according to Red West, "he unleashed the hurricane."

It was merely the beginning. The response to Elvis' initial appearance was unheard of. Shortly afterwards, girls from all over the country swooned at the mere mention of Presley's name. His fan mail increased considerably, and for the first time, The Dorsey Brothers' ratings picked up.

America blew a gasket. Suddenly, Elvis was labeled as "perversely obscene," due mostly to his sexual acrobatics while performing. The nation's holy, religious and moral citizens widely objected to Elvis doing "what was reserved exclusively for the bedroom."

Above and below: Presley was frequently honored by heads of state.

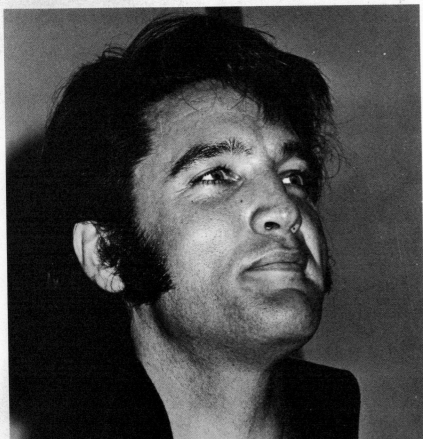

The controversy, over the following weeks, blossomed. Presley was dubbed "Elvis the Pelvis," and it was rumored that he was a new threat to American virtue. At a time when porno films and the entire sexual revolution were unheard of, Elvis created more than a ripple. All over the country, students were expelled from high school for refusing to cut their duck-tail type haircuts. Girls wrote in, saying that they would commit suicide if Elvis didn't meet them. Newspaper articles proclaimed that the high decibel level of Elvis' music could deafen the youth of America. Rock and roll dances were banned in many American cities.

Most of the negative reaction surprised Presley, who said at the time, "Heck, I just go the way I feel. There ain't nothing bad about it. I would never do it if I thought it was bad. There is nothing planned in this. It's just music

It was merely another beginning, as the best was yet to come.

Merchandising executives were quick to jump on the Presley bandwagon, and pretty soon there were Presley T-shirts, Presley jeans, Elvis Presley lipstick, bubble gum, footballs, shirts, socks, sweatshirts, pajamas, ballpoint pens and dairies, to name a few.

There was more though.

As Colonel Tom Parker sat back and basked in the knowledge that his old school techniques for promoting an act proved worthwhile again. Elvis Presley fan clubs started popping up all over the world. At one point, there was reported to be some one million card carrying members of the Elvis Presley Fan Club.

Meanwhile, Hollywood was preparing for the arrival of Elvis "The King" Presley.

Above: In 1970, Elvis was one of the Ten Outstanding Young Men of America.

Below: In 1969, The King signed for a four week engagement at the MGM Grand Hotel, in Las Vegas.

and singing, that's all."

Elvis' mother, Gladys Presley, echoed her son's statements. She would fly off the handle at the slightest suggestion that her son's act was in any way vulgar or obscene. "My boy wouldn't do anything bad," she said, "nothing bad at all. He is a good boy, a boy that's never forgotten his church upbringing and he hasn't changed one bit."

A guest shot on *The Steve Allen Show* and Elvis singing *Hound Dog* was more or less what made Ed Sullivan take notice. Steve Allen's ratings climbed steadily by having Elvis on the show, and although Sullivan seemed less than fond of Presley, he knew what he wanted, and needed. Sullivan paid a record fifteen thousand dollars for one appearance, three times what he'd paid even top performers. It was perhaps Parker's way of making Sullivan eat his words.

THE HIT RECORDS

In his unprecedented career, Elvis sold more than 400,000,000 records! Individually, he had forty-five hit records that sold more than a million each. Just in case you can't name 'em all, here's the complete list of the golden disks:

1. Heartbreak Hotel
2. I Was The One
3. I Want You, I Need You, I Love You
4. Hound Dog
5. Don't Be Cruel
6. Love Me Tender
7. Any Way You Want Me (That's How I Will Be)
8. Too Much
9. Playing For Keeps
10. All Shook Up
11. That's When Your Heartaches Begin
12. Loving You
13. (Let Me Be Your) Teddy Bear
14. Jailhouse Rock
15. Treat Me Nice
16. Don't
17. I Beg Of You
18. Wear My Ring Around Your Neck
19. Hard Headed Woman
20. I Got Stung
21. It's Now Or Never
22. A Mess Of Blues
23. Are You Lonesome Tonight?
24. I Gotta Know
25. Can't Help Falling In Love
26. Rock-A-Hula Baby
27. Return To Sender

Above: The King sweats heavily during a Las Vegas engagement.

Above: Elvis in 1970, a little more subdued than usual.

Above: In 1970, Elvis was the subject of an MGM documentary.

The King performing before a packed house at the Houston Astrodome, circa 1970.

Elvis with another biggie, Fats Domino.

THE IMITATORS

When Elvis was drafted into the Army, the entire female population of the world went into mourning. Every step of Elvis' induction was filmed. His famous haircut, being fitted for his uniform and his six week training period. Some skeptics thought with Elvis gone for two years his fame would die. On the contrary, his record label had enough material to release while he was in the army to keep him from being forgotten. Elvis received more mail than any other soldier in history. The girls loved him and counted the days until his return.

In the meantime, a new production company found a way to capitalize on Elvis' induction: A play called *Bye Bye Birdie*. The fictional character walked, talked and moved his hips like the real Presley, and he too was being drafted into the Army.

The play, for those of you who don't remember it, later became a movie. The plot was simple. Once Conrad Birdie's publicity people found out he was going into the Army they decided upon a scheme that would clinch his popularity. They would pick at random a girl from his fan club, and bring her on the Ed Sullivan show to be kissed by the famed Birdie. His so-called last kiss until he returned to his fans two years later. The play starred, Dick Van Dyke, Paul Lynde, Chita Rivera, Michael J. Pollard, and Dick Gautier, as Birdie. It was an instant success and had a long run on Broadway, never for one minute letting Elvis' fans forget him.

Although Gautier had Presley's personality down pat, he wasn't the only imitator. Many hopefuls tried to fill Elvis' shoes, Frankie Avelon, Dion and the Belmonts, Fabian, Frankie Valli, and others now long forgotten. Each one of them had his stay at the top, but not for long. They just didn't have the magic Elvis did. And when he returned in 1960, he was hotter than ever.

But in the 60's, Elvis found that musical taste had changed somewhat. The popular music of that time was not as frantic as his had been, the so-called "Elvis Pelvis" didn't need his hip-shaking gyrations to get through to the ladies. He put less emphasis on his rock numbers and put more of himself into his romantic ballads. To complete the change in image, he even cut off his sideburns.

Elvis took almost eight years out from touring to continue to turn out hit records, and his movies came out regularly and made big money. But as the 60's wore on, especially after the Beatles, whose self-proclaimed goal had been to surpass Elvis as the king of rock and roll, it had begun to look as if time and popular taste were at last passing Presly by.

Then Elvis went on tour in 1968, riding the wave of renewed interest in 1950's rock and roll—and he was bigger than ever!

Forty-five of Elvis' top records sold over one million copies and a grand total of 400 million copies of his recordings have been sold to date!

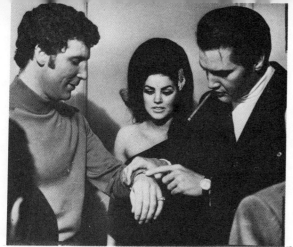

Above: Elvis compares watches with friend Tom Jones as wife Priscilla looks on.

Right: A publicity shot from 1962

The King with Barbara Stanwyck in *Roustabout*.

Presley was known for wearing bandanas, as far back as high school.

Elvis Presley and his trained hands.

The Pelvis kisses a starry-eyed fan.

In the sixties, The King stuck mainly to records and films.

A haggard Presley signs autographs despite his fatigue.

Elvis is flanked by his bodyguards Red West and Dave Hebler.

HIS LATER YEARS

Three of Elvis Presley's former bodyguards have, for the first time, told everything about the king of Rock and Roll in a book called *Elvis. . . . What Happened?*

It is one of the frankest, most sensational books ever written about any famous personality: the bodyguards reveal everything.

Elvis asked one of the guards to arrange the execution of a Karate instructor, Mike Stone, who just happened to have run off with Elvis' wife, Priscilla.

He was also infatuated with guns and would often shoot a bullet or two at the television set if he wasn't pleased at what was on t.v.

He also shot through a bathroom wall, missing by hairs his girl friend, Linda Thompson.

At another time, he was in a fit of rage and hurled a pool cue at a girl fan, hitting her viciously in the chest. The girl was stunned, but all was hushed up.

The book also talks about his obsession with drugs, nearly killing a girl he was with. They were both unconscious in bed.

I guess you're all interested in who really did rat on Elvis. The names of the bodyguards are Red West, 41, a childhood friend of Presley's; Sonny West, 38, Red's cousin, a friend and bodyguard for fourteen years; and Dave Hebler, 38, a karate instructor and Presley's bodyguard since 1974.

They were all more than just guards. They were Presley's confidantes, advisors and close personal friends, or the "Memphis Mafia" as Presley liked to think of them. They frequently sat up through the night keeping their lonely idol company when he felt most depressed.

In times of trouble, they were the only ones Elvis felt he could talk to, and always turn to for help with his girlfriends, his pills, his over-excited fans.

Their close friendship with Elvis came to an abrupt end in July of last year when he fired them. Elvis was a Jekyll and Hyde, he was capable of enormous generosity and terrifying rages.

The book almost parallels Elvis to a Howard Hughes type figure, a superstar who has been forced into a hermit's existence by his bizarre habits and lifestyle.

It was so different in his early days of fame. Elvis was generous with his hospitality. His houses were continual halfway stops for his cronies and the ever faithful band of Southerners who had been dubbed by the press the "Memphis Mafia."

If Elvis liked you, you were in, and when Elvis liked you, there were no half measures. Clothes, parties, Cadillacs, were all part of the accoutrements of being a friend.

One night though when Elvis celebrated the end of filming *Fun in Acapulco*, his friends saw his other side. Sonny West had taken two girls to Presley's house in Bel Air.

Sonny told Dunleavy: "One of the girls later became quite a well-known actress, and the other one, who will remain nameless, was a sweet little thing. Depending on what sort of mood he was in, Elvis might say hello to everybody and go straight to bed. Other nights he wouldn't even come down at all. But if he was looking around for a little action, he would sweet talk some gal for a while and then take her upstairs for some action.

Right: Elvis the Pelvis busy at what he does best—singing.

On this particular night, Elvis didn't seem to be doing any of these things. He was pretty tired and seemed a bit agitated.

He wanted Sonny to play pool with him. Sonny had these ladies with him, but when Elvis wanted to do something you'd better do it.

So Sonny left the girls and all the other vultures up there and started to play pool with Elvis.

Elvis' mood was not being helped by the fact that he was muffing every second shot. Sonny got a bit tense, knowing that Elvis can flash in these situations. One of the two girls got bored waiting for Sonny and left.

Elvis was just ready to hit a shot when the girl came down the stairs to say goodbye. She asked Sonny to move his car because it was blocking hers.

Sonny asked her to wait a second, when Elvis rose from the table where he was about to hit a shot and started screaming at Sonny to have someone else move the car since he was busy.

The girl apologized for bothering them, but again that wasn't enough for Elvis. He stood there glaring at her, and when she asked Sonny to please move his car again, being frightened to death of Elvis and wanting to get out of there as fast as she could, he turned around and speared her with the pool cue right in her right breast.

She didn't scream. It was more like a sharp little gasp, and she crumpled backwards on the floor.

Sonny dashed around the table to where the girl lay on the ground. Sonny kept asking her if she was okay.

Presley picked up another cue, screaming that she was fine and just trying to be dramatic. He shouted to Sonny to drag her out of his house. Sonny gently picked the girl up and carried her into another room. Eventually she recovered and drove home.

But Elvis was insistent that he had a right to do what he did because she neglected to listen to his first command and when he told her to go away she called him a son of a bitch. He didn't think it was right.

One of the book's most startling revelations is about Elvis' drug habits. It was one of the best guarded secrets.

He always took pills to go to sleep. He took pills to get up. He took pills to go to the john and he took pills to stop himself from going to the john.

There have been times where he was so hyper on uppers that he had trouble breathing and on one occasion he thought he was going to die.

He was a walking pharmaceutical shop, according to his former employees. He had smoked marijuana, but didn't like to smoke because it burned his throat. He took uppers and downers and all sorts of very strong painkillers, like Percodan and the stuff they give terminal cancer patients.

He had often gotten prescriptions in the names of a lot of the staff. From time to time he had a doctor who used to make up his prescriptions, but who has since vanished.

A lot of Elvis' close friends thought he was committing suicide slowly with the drug taking. It may have turned out to be true.

Elvis was one of the few men in the world who could have had anything he wanted. He was one of the most popular personalities, even though he never played Europe because he was afraid to fly. He could have been a fantastic physical specimen.

It is hard to believe that he became fat and decided he didn't care about life. Did he deliberately set out to destroy himself? Was he bent on death?

All three bodyguards have seen Presley in a complete stupor from pills. There had been actual shows he had done that he didn't even remember.

Sometimes he got up there and talked and talked to the audience instead of singing. He would give his philosophy on life and it was very boring. People didn't come to hear him talk, they came to hear him sing.

One night he did a Karate exhibition for 28 minutes straight in Las Vegas. People were walking out all over the place, and Vegas still offered him $200,000 a week to perform there.

Sometimes he'd forget the sequence of songs, and he would forget the lyrics to songs. Other times there were songs scheduled to be sung, and he would just refuse to do them. But all in all, Elvis was one of the best performers in the business. When he was straight, and slimmed down, working on his own energy, there was no showman like him on earth.

Above: Elvis arrives at the wedding of Sonny West, his bodyguard.

The one and only King loved the electricity of an audience.

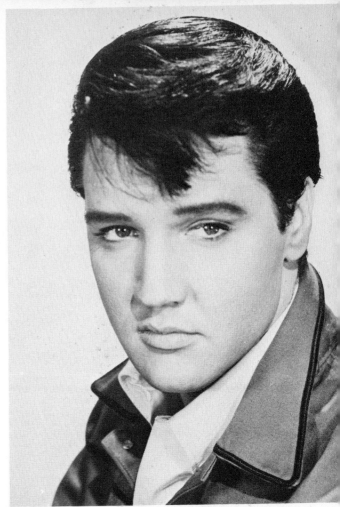
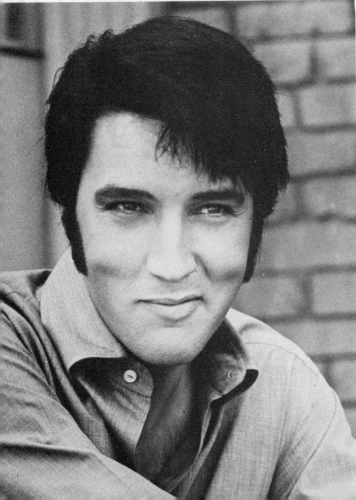

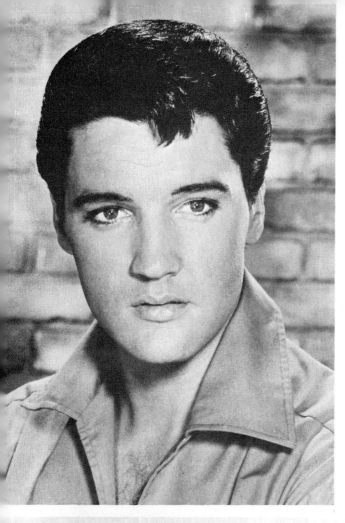

ELVIS : BIG

Elvis Presley's death is almost as big a business as was his life.

Upon hearing of his untimely demise, his fans, trivia buffs, trivia and memorabilia collectors have rushed into stores, stripping the shelves clean of every last Elvis item, such as records, posters and books on the late, great King of Rock and Roll.

Only one day after Elvis' death, some 250,000 copies of his swansong, his last album *Moody Blue*, were sold. RCA, which released the record, immediately began working its staff around the clock to meet the sudden demand for the album. Before Elvis' death, the album was selling some hundred thousand copies per week. Suddenly, things were a bit different.

Presley had been with RCA since 1956, when Colonel Tom Parker, the man really responsible for Elvis hitting the big time, sold them The King's recording contract for $35,000. By 1975, Elvis had sold some five hundred million records. His death will ultimately push sales up to six hundred million, said a spokesman for RCA.

"They took everything and anything," said one record store manager in New York City. "There were fifty people waiting outside the store this morning (the day after The King's death) when we opened the store."

In San Diego, California, a clerk at one record store claimed, "We sold out Elvis' new album within an hour after his death was reported. An old gray haired couple bought the last copy we had."

A huge rush was predicted on Presley Books by Ballantine Books, who that very week, ironically enough, released *Elvis:*

What Happened?, written by Presley's former friends and bodyguards, Red West, Dave Hebler and Sonny West, Red's brother. Some 400,000 copies had been printed with orders for a mere 250,000 before Elvis' death. When it was reported, according to a spokesman, orders soon doubled and then tripled.

Even in death, Elvis will still reign as the King, now and forever.

BUSINESS

Below: Word of the King's death brought a rush of record buyers all over the world.

THE KING IS DEAD

It's needless to add "long live the King," because it's absolutely guaranteed that Elvis will live on in the memory of millions as the one-and-only King of Rock & Roll!

It was a dark, dismal day in Tennessee when The King was laid to rest. That had nothing to do with the weather, but rather the mood of the immense crowd that came from near and far to both witness the extraordinary event and pay their final homage to the man who brought them thrills, tears, chills, rushes and gushes over a twenty-year period. For some, it was as if *their* world had ended!

The crowd—mob, to be more precise—was alternately sedate and hysterical. Memories of The Pelvis grinding out *Hound Dog*, Elvis begging *Love Me Tender* and Mr. Rock stomping through *Jailhouse Rock* floated among the throngs. Everyone had his or her own favorite, and they all added up to perhaps the greatest adulation ever paid an American singing star. His appeal was not limited to any one group—as his fellow stars' testimonials had indicated. From Frank Sinatra to Cher, Elvis was the one, above all, who most influenced both the music and the culture of the times.

Yes, The King is dead, but his memory will long live on. One of Elvis' more esoteric songs talked about being "tired and so weary, but I must keep travellin' on, 'til the Lord comes to guide me . . . travellin' on." The King is travellin' on. . . .and will be in the minds of millions for years to come.

TRAGEDY!

The hysteria reached such a fever pitch as the throngs of Presley mourners flocked to Graceland that tragedy struck, amidst the mourning.

As mobs of mourners covered every inch of space outside of Elvis' home, suddenly an automobile went out of control and hurtled into a portion of the horrified crowd. As if the death of The King wasn't enough—now two more people were killed while innocently mourning their lost hero.

It was truly tragedy upon tragedy!

Above: Friends kneel over the body of a girl who was hit by a speeding car that barreled through Elvis's fans outside his mansion, while a stream of vehicles (right) follow another stream of Cadillac limos as far as the eye can see.

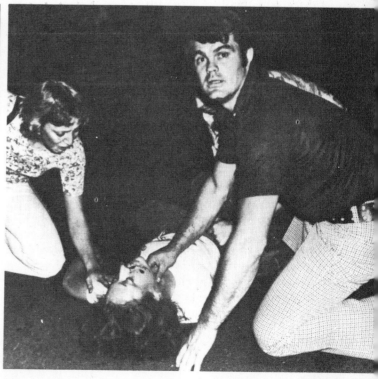

THE FINAL GOODBYE

"My sister and I just came for the day," said one grief-stricken fan, a receptionist from Houston, Texas, "but we had to do it. Our little bit for his memory. He was The King."

She was far from the only one who felt this way. In fact, there were some thirty thousand people who felt exactly the same way, and turned out to catch one last glimpse of the man they had proclaimed their king, back in 1956.

"He reached out with his music and he took hold of so many people's lives," someone else was quoted as saying. "Every man wanted to be like him," said another onlooker, adding "and he was every woman's dream."

Throughout the day, August 17, over one hundred thousand people turned out to see Elvis for the last time. In Graceland, the name of Elvis's huge estate in Memphis, fans were quiet and, according to police, "impeccably well behaved," although two arrests were made, and one over-zealous fan drove a car through the throngs of people, killing two girls and injuring another.

Many in the crowd had waited all night to view the body. Their cars lined the highway. The restaurants in the vicinity were thriving with business.

In death, just as in life, Elvis had tight security.

Above: Ann-Margret and hubby-manager Roger Smith leaving Elvis's funeral.

"Please don't say he was fat," sobbed a fan from Memphis, who was crying uncontrollably after viewing Elvis' body at Graceland. "They made him look fat in that coffin," Mary claimed. "People must know he doesn't look like this." Elvis weighed some two hundred pounds at the time of is demise.

Clutching a picture of a younger and slimmer Elvis Presley, the same fan commented, "This is what he really looks like."

One lifelong fan, together with his brothers, drove some twelve hours, still clad in their baseball uniforms, just for that last view. "We came off the field yesterday evening," he said, "and heard he was dead. There was no question about it. We stopped to get money for gas and took off. He was the man. He was it. We had tickets for a concert he was going to give next month. We figured, he didn't come to see us, so we came to see him."

HOW HIS MUSICAL PEERS SAW HIM

All of show business was shocked upon hearing of Elvis' death. It's interesting to note some of the praiseworthy comments made in the nation's press by stars as diverse as Frank Sinatra and The Beach Boys' Carl Wilson.

ROY ORBISON: "Elvis was the kindest man you could ever wish to meet. I last saw Elvis in February when I took some friends backstage to meet him. They were all impressed with his kindness and sincerity. He was the innovator of modern music, and he opened the doors for a lot of people after him."

CHER ALLMAN: "It's an incredible tragedy. The first concert I attended was an Elvis Presley concert when I was eleven years old. Even at that age he made me realize the tremendous effect a performer could have on an audience."

PAT BOONE: "Elvis was truly The King. A lot of us wondered what an old Elvis would be like. Now we will never know."

FRANK SINATRA: "We lost a good friend today."

BEACH BOYS' CARL WILSON; "His music was the only thing exclusively ours. His wasn't my mom and dad's music. His voice was a total miracle, a true miracle in the music business."